TELL ME THE TRUTH ABOUT LOVE

Tell Me the Truth About Love

Fifteen poems by
W. H. AUDEN

faber and faber

First published in 1994
by Faber and Faber Limited
3 Queen Square London WC1N 3AU
Enlarged edition 1998

This selection of poems
reprinted from *Collected Poems*
by W. H. Auden, revised edition 1991

Phototypeset by Parker Typesetting Service, Leicester
Printed and bound in Great Britain by
Mackays of Chatham PLC, Chatham, Kent

A CIP record for this book
is available from the British Library

ISBN 0 571 195938

6 8 10 9 7 5

Contents

TELL ME THE TRUTH
ABOUT LOVE

O Tell Me the Truth About Love

Some say that love's a little boy,
     And some say it's a bird,
Some say it makes the world go round,
     And some say that's absurd,
And when I asked the man next door,
     Who looked as if he knew,
His wife got very cross indeed,
     And said it wouldn't do.

    Does it look like a pair of pyjamas,
      Or the ham in a temperance hotel?
    Does its odour remind one of llamas,
      Or has it a comforting smell?
    Is it prickly to touch as a hedge is,
      Or soft as eiderdown fluff?
    Is it sharp or quite smooth at the edges?
      O tell me the truth about love.

Our history books refer to it
     In cryptic little notes,
It's quite a common topic on
     The Transatlantic boats;
I've found the subject mentioned in
     Accounts of suicides,
And even seen it scribbled on
     The backs of railway-guides.

    Does it howl like a hungry Alsatian,
      Or boom like a military band?
    Could one give a first-rate imitation
      On a saw or a Steinway Grand?

Is its singing at parties a riot?
    Does it only like Classical stuff?
Will it stop when one wants to be quiet?
    O tell me the truth about love.

I looked inside the summer-house,
        It wasn't ever there,
I tried the Thames at Maidenhead,
        And Brighton's bracing air,
I don't know what the blackbird sang,
        Or what the tulip said;
But it wasn't in the chicken-run,
        Or underneath the bed.

Can it pull extraordinary faces?
    Is it usually sick on a swing?
Does it spend all its time at the races,
    Or fiddling with pieces of string?
Has it views of its own about money?
    Does it think Patriotism enough?
Are its stories vulgar but funny?
    O tell me the truth about love.

When it comes, will it come without warning,
    Just as I'm picking my nose?
Will it knock on my door in the morning,
    Or tread in the bus on my toes?
Will it come like a change in the weather?
    Will its greeting be courteous or rough?
Will it alter my life altogether?
    O tell me the truth about love.

January 1938

Song

Fish in the unruffled lakes
Their swarming colours wear,
Swans in the winter air
A white perfection have,
And the great lion walks
Through his innocent grove;
Lion, fish and swan
Act, and are gone
Upon Time's toppling wave.

We, till shadowed days are done,
We must weep and sing
Duty's conscious wrong,
The Devil in the clock,
The goodness carefully worn
For atonement or for luck;
We must lose our loves,
On each beast and bird that moves
Turn an envious look.

Sighs for folly done and said
Twist our narrow days,
But I must bless, I must praise
That you, my swan, who have
All gifts that to the swan
Impulsive Nature gave,
The majesty and pride,
Last night should add
Your voluntary love.

March 1936

Underneath an Abject Willow

Underneath an abject willow,
    Lover, sulk no more
Act from thought should quickly follow.
    What is thinking for?
Your unique and moping station
    Proves you cold;
    Stand up and fold
Your map of desolation.

Bells that toll across the meadows
    From the sombre spire
Toll for these unloving shadows
    Love does not require.
All that lives may love; why longer
    Bow to loss
    With arms across?
Strike and you shall conquer.

Geese in flocks above you flying,
    Their direction know,
Icy brooks beneath you flowing,
    To their ocean go.
Dark and dull is your distraction:
    Walk then, come,
    No longer numb
Into your satisfaction.

March 1936

Calypso

Dríver drive fáster and máke a good rún
Down the Spríngfield Line únder the shíning sún.

Flý like an aéroplane, dón't pull up shórt
Till you bráke for Grand Céntral Státion, New Yórk.

For thére in the míddle of thát waiting-háll
Should be stánding the óne that Í love best of áll.

If he's nót there to méet me when Í get to tówn,
I'll stánd on the síde-walk with téars rolling dówn.

For hé is the óne that I lóve to look ón,
The ácme of kindness and pérfectión.

He présses my hánd and he sáys he loves mé,
Which I índ an admiráble pecúliaritý.

The wóods are bright gréen on both sídes of the líne;
The trées have their lóves though they're dífferent from míne.

But the póor fat old bánker in the sún-parlour cár
Has nó one to lóve him excépt his cigár.

If Í were the Héad of the Chúrch or the Státe,
I'd pówder my nóse and just téll them to wáit.

For lóve's more impórtant and pówerful thán
Even a príest or a pólitíciàn.

May 1939

Warm are the Still and Lucky Miles

Warm are the still and lucky miles,
White shores of longing stretch away,
A light of recognition fills
   The whole great day, and bright
The tiny world of lovers' arms.

Silence invades the breathing wood
Where drowsy limbs a treasure keep,
Now greenly falls the learned shade
   Across the sleeping brows
And stirs their secret to a smile.

Restored! Returned! The lost are borne
On seas of shipwreck home at last:
See! In a fire of praising burns
   The dry dumb past, and we
Our life-day long shall part no more.

October 1939

Carry Her Over the Water

Carry her over the water,
   And set her down under the tree,
Where the culvers white all day and all night,
   And the winds from every quarter,
Sing agreeably, agreeably, agreeably of love.

Put a gold ring on her finger,
   And press her close to your heart,
While the fish in the lake their snapshots take,
   And the frog, that sanguine singer,
Sings agreeably, agreeably, agreeably of love.

The streets shall all flock to your marriage,
   The houses turn round to look,
The tables and chairs say suitable prayers,
   And the horses drawing your carriage
Sing agreeably, agreeably, agreeably of love.

? 1939

Deftly, Admiral, Cast Your Fly

Deftly, admiral, cast your fly
    Into the slow deep hover,
Till the wise old trout mistake and die;
    Salt are the deeps that cover
    The glittering fleets you led,
      White is your head.

Read on, ambassador, engrossed
    In your favorite Stendhal;
The Outer Provinces are lost,
    Unshaven horsemen swill
    The great wines of the Chateaux
      Where you danced long ago.

Do not turn, do not lift your eyes
    Toward the still pair standing
On the bridge between your properties,
    Indifferent to your minding:
    In its glory, in its power,
      This is their hour.

Nothing your strength, your skill, could do
    Can alter their embrace
Or dispersuade the Furies who
    At the appointed place
    With claw and dreadful brow
      Wait for them now.

June 1948

As I Walked Out One Evening

As I walked out one evening,
   Walking down Bristol Street,
The crowds upon the pavement
   Were fields of harvest wheat.

And down by the brimming river
   I heard a lover sing
Under an arch of the railway:
   'Love has no ending.

'I'll love you, dear, I'll love you
   Till China and Africa meet,
And the river jumps over the mountain
   And the salmon sing in the street.

'I'll love you till the ocean
   Is folded and hung up to dry
And the seven stars go squawking
   Like geese about the sky.

'The years shall run like rabbits,
   For in my arms I hold
The Flower of the Ages,
   And the first love of the world.'

But all the clocks in the city
   Began to whirr and chime:
'O let not Time deceive you,
   You cannot conquer Time.

'In the burrows of the Nightmare
    Where Justice naked is,
Time watches from the shadow
    And coughs when you would kiss.

'In headaches and in worry
    Vaguely life leaks away,
And Time will have his fancy
    To-morrow or to-day.

'Into many a green valley
    Drifts the appalling snow;
Time breaks the threaded dances
    And the diver's brilliant bow.

'O plunge your hands in water,
    Plunge them in up to the wrist;
Stare, stare in the basin
    And wonder what you've missed.

'The glacier knocks in the cupboard,
    The desert sighs in the bed,
And the crack in the tea-cup opens
    A lane to the land of the dead.

'Where the beggars raffle the banknotes
    And the Giant is enchanting to Jack,
And the Lily-white Boy is a Roarer,
    And Jill goes down on her back.

'O look, look in the mirror,
    O look in your distress;
Life remains a blessing
    Although you cannot bless.

'O stand, stand at the window
    As the tears scald and start;
You will love your crooked neighbour
    With your crooked heart.'

It was late, late in the evening,
    The lovers they were gone;
The clocks had ceased their chiming,
    And the deep river ran on.

                    November 1937

Lullaby

Lay your sleeping head, my love,
Human on my faithless arm;
Time and fevers burn away
Individual beauty from
Thoughtful children, and the grave
Proves the child ephemeral:
But in my arms till break of day
Let the living creature lie,
Mortal, guilty, but to me
The entirely beautiful.

Soul and body have no bounds:
To lovers as they lie upon
Her tolerant enchanted slope
In their ordinary swoon,
Grave the vision Venus sends
Of supernatural sympathy,
Universal love and hope;
While an abstract insight wakes
Among the glaciers and the rocks
The hermit's carnal ecstasy.

Certainty, fidelity
On the stroke of midnight pass
Like vibrations of a bell
And fashionable madmen raise
Their pedantic boring cry:
Every farthing of the cost,
All the dreaded cards foretell,
Shall be paid, but from this night
Not a whisper, not a thought,
Not a kiss nor look be lost.

Beauty, midnight, vision dies;
Let the winds of dawn that blow
Softly round your dreaming head
Such a day of welcome show
Eye and knocking heart may bless,
Find our mortal world enough;
Noons of dryness find you fed
By the involuntary powers,
Nights of insult let you pass
Watched by every human love.

January 1937

Let a Florid Music Praise

Let a florid music praise,
   The flute and the trumpet,
Beauty's conquest of your face:
In that land of flesh and bone,
Where from citadels on high
Her imperial standards fly,
     Let the hot sun
     Shine on, shine on.

O but the unloved have had power,
   The weeping and striking,
Always: time will bring their hour;
Their secretive children walk
Through your vigilance of breath
To unpardonable Death,
     And my vows break
     Before his look.

February 1936

At Last the Secret is Out

At last the secret is out, as it always must come in the end,
The delicious story is ripe to tell to the intimate friend;
Over the tea-cups and in the square the tongue has its desire;
Still waters run deep, my dear, there's never smoke without fire.

Behind the corpse in the reservoir, behind the ghost on the links,
Behind the lady who dances and the man who madly drinks,
Under the look of fatigue, the attack of migraine and the sigh
There is always another story, there is more than meets the eye.

For the clear voice suddenly singing, high up in the convent wall,
The scent of the elder bushes, the sporting prints in the hall,
The croquet matches in summer, the handshake, the cough, the kiss,
There is always a wicked secret, a private reason for this.

April 1936

O What is That Sound

O what is that sound which so thrills the ear
   Down in the valley drumming, drumming?
Only the scarlet soldiers, dear,
   The soldiers coming.

O what is that light I see flashing so clear
   Over the distance brightly, brightly?
Only the sun on their weapons, dear,
   As they step lightly.

O what are they doing with all that gear,
   What are they doing this morning, this morning?
Only their usual manoeuvres, dear,
   Or perhaps a warning.

O why have they left the road down there,
   Why are they suddenly wheeling, wheeling?
Perhaps a change in their orders, dear.
   Why are you kneeling?

O haven't they stopped for the doctor's care,
   Haven't they reined their horses, their horses?
Why, they are none of them wounded, dear,
   None of these forces.

O is it the parson they want, with white hair,
   Is it the parson, is it, is it?
No, they are passing his gateway, dear,
   Without a visit.

O it must be the farmer who lives so near.
    It must be the farmer so cunning, so cunning?
They have passed the farmyard already, dear,
    And now they are running.

O where are you going? Stay with me here!
    Were the vows you swore deceiving, deceiving?
No, I promised to love you, dear,
    But I must be leaving.

O it's broken the lock and splintered the door,
    O it's the gate where they're turning, turning;
Their boots are heavy on the floor
    And their eyes are burning.

October 1932

Eyes Look Into the Well

Eyes look into the well,
Tears run down from the eye;
The tower cracked and fell
From the quiet winter sky.

Under a midnight stone
Love was buried by thieves;
The robbed heart begs for a bone,
The damned rustle like leaves.

Face down in the flooded brook
With nothing more to say,
Lies One the soldiers took,
And spoiled and threw away.

1940

Johnny

O the valley in the summer where I and my John
Beside the deep river would walk on and on
While the flowers at our feet and the birds up above
Argued so sweetly on reciprocal love,
And I leaned on his shoulder; 'O Johnny, let's play':
But he frowned like thunder and he went away.

O that Friday near Christmas as I well recall
When we went to the Charity Matinee Ball,
The floor was so smooth and the band was so loud
And Johnny so handsome I felt so proud;
'Squeeze me tighter, dear Johnny, let's dance till it's day':
But he frowned like thunder and he went away.

Shall I ever forget at the Grand Opera
When music poured out of each wonderful star?
Diamonds and pearls they hung dazzling down
Over each silver or golden silk gown;
'O John I'm in heaven,' I whispered to say:
But he frowned like thunder and he went away.

O but he was as fair as a garden in flower,
As slender and tall as the great Eiffel Tower,
When the waltz throbbed out on the long promenade
O his eyes and his smile they went straight to my heart;
'O marry me, Johnny, I'll love and obey':
But he frowned like thunder and he went away.

O last night I dreamed of you, Johnny, my lover,
You'd the sun on one arm and the moon on the other,
The sea it was blue and the grass it was green,
Every star rattled a round tambourine;
Ten thousand miles deep in a pit there I lay:
But you frowned like thunder and you went away.

April 1937

Funeral Blues

Stop all the clocks, cut off the telephone,
Prevent the dog from barking with a juicy bone,
Silence the pianos and with muffled drum
Bring out the coffin, let the mourners come.

Let aeroplanes circle moaning overhead
Scribbling on the sky the message He Is Dead,
Put crêpe bows round the white necks of the public doves,
Let the traffic policemen wear black cotton gloves.

He was my North, my South, my East and West,
My working week and my Sunday rest,
My noon, my midnight, my talk, my song;
I thought that love would last for ever: I was wrong.

The stars are not wanted now; put out every one;
Pack up the moon and dismantle the sun;
Pour away the ocean and sweep up the wood;
For nothing now can ever come to any good.

April 1936

About W. H. Auden

Wystan Hugh Auden was born in York on 21 February 1907. He studied at Gresham's School, Holt, and Christ Church, Oxford, after which he lived for a year in a Berlin slum. In the early thirties he taught at Helensburgh, in Scotland, and then at the Downs School, near Malvern. In the later thirties he worked as a freelance writer, and published travel books on Iceland (with Louis Mac-Neice) and the Sino–Japanese War (with Christopher Isherwood). Also in collaboration with Isherwood, he wrote three plays for the Group Theatre: *The Dog Beneath the Skin, The Ascent of F6*, and *On the Frontier*. In 1939 he left England for the United States, where he became a citizen in 1946. In America he lived in New York until 1941, then taught at Michigan and Swarthmore. In 1945 he served in Germany with the US Strategic Bombing Survey, and, when he returned, again took an apartment in New York. From 1948 to 1972 he spent his winters in America and his summers in Europe, first in Ischia, then, from 1958, in a house he owned in Kirchstetten, Austria. During this period he wrote four opera libretti with Chester Kallman: *The Rake's Progress* (for Igor Stravinsky), *Elegy for Young Lovers* and *The Bassarids* (both for Hans Werner Henze), and *Love's Labour's Lost* (for Nicolas Nabokov). From 1956 to 1960 he spent a few months of each year in Oxford as the elected Professor of Poetry. In 1972 he left his winter home in New York to return to Oxford. He died in Vienna on 29 September 1973.

*Books by W. H. Auden
available from Faber and Faber*

Collected Poems
Selected Poems
Collected Shorter Poems
Collected Longer Poems
The English Auden:
Poems, Essays & Dramatic Writings
Auden's Juvenilia
As I Walked Out One Evening
Paul Bunyan
A Certain World:
A Commonplace Book
The Enchafèd Flood
Secondary Worlds
The Dyer's Hand
Prose 1926–1938:
Essays and Reviews and Travel Books in Prose and Verse

with Christopher Isherwood
Plays and Other Dramatic Writings
by W. H. Auden 1928–1938
The Dog Beneath the Skin
The Ascent of F6
and On the Frontier
Journey to a War

with Chester Kallman
Libretti and Other Dramatic Writings
by W. H. Auden 1939–1973

with Louis MacNeice
Letters from Iceland

with Paul Taylor
Norse Poems

with Leif Sjöberg
Markings by Dag Hammarskjöld

with Louis Kronenberger
The Faber Book of Aphorisms

by Alan Ansen
The Table Talk of W. H. Auden